Crock Pot Cookbook for Two

Crock Pot Cookbook for Two

1000-Day Fabulous and Fuss-Free Crock Pot Recipes Designed for Two People

Winda Zarsen

TABLE OF CONTENTS

CHAPTER 5: POULTRY 058

CHAPTER 6: BEEF, PORK AND LAMB.............................073

INTRODUCTION

You want wholesome and delicious meals but you just don't have the time to prepare them after a long day at work. Most crock pot cookbooks offer recipes for a crowd and you don't want leftovers taking up space in the fridge. This crock pot cookbook is different. The perfect gift for newlyweds, elderly couples, or anyone who is too busy to spend hours futzing in the kitchen, these recipes will put just the right amount of home-cooked food on your table with little time and effort on your part.

Use this crock pot cookbook for instructions every time you get cooking. These crock pot recipes do not only taste good, but they also look appetizing and include every possible variation of your family's favorite meals you might have tried elsewhere. Combine ingredients and crock pot recipes as you want to get a perfect family dinner.

Learn how simple it is to cook tasty and healthy meals using only a crock pot and around half an hour of your free time. Spare no more, prepare your ingredients and the crock pot will do the rest!

Cheers!

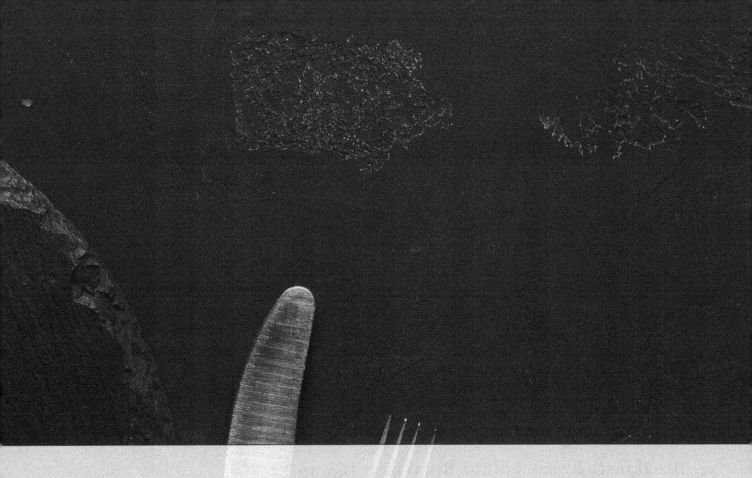

CHAPTER 1: 30-DAY MEAL PLAN

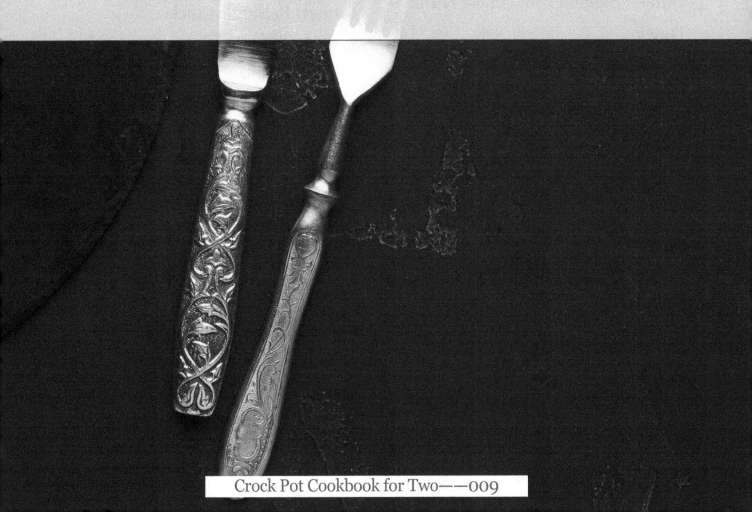

Day 1

Breakfast: Bacon, Egg & Kale Casserole
Lunch: Zucchini Lasagna
Dinner: Meatballs

Day 2

Breakfast: Breakfast Sausage
Lunch: Shrimp Boil
Dinner: Balsamic Chicken

Day 3

Breakfast: Garlic Sausage with Egg & Broccoli Bake
Lunch: Stuffed Taco Peppers
Dinner: Beef Curry

Day 4

Breakfast: Sweet Potato Breakfast Casserole
Lunch: Ranch Chicken
Dinner: Salmon with Lemon & Dill

Day 5

Breakfast: Breakfast Casserole
Lunch: Beef Pot Roast
Dinner: Stewed Veggies

Day 6

Breakfast: Bacon, Egg & Kale Casserole
Lunch: Lamb Shanks with Green Beans
Dinner: Sesame Ginger Chicken

Day 7

Breakfast: Sausage & Broccoli Breakfast Casserole
Lunch: Zucchini Lasagna
Dinner: Shrimp Scampi

Day 8

Breakfast: Bacon & Egg Breakfast
Lunch: Cauliflower Pizza

Dinner: Salmon with Lemon & Dill

Day 9

Breakfast: Breakfast Bake
Lunch: Mongolian Beef
Dinner: Sesame Ginger Chicken

Day 10

Breakfast: Cauliflower Hash Browns
Lunch: Lamb with Thyme
Dinner: Salmon with Lemon Cream Sauce

Day 11

Breakfast: Breakfast Casserole
Lunch: Shrimp Jambalaya
Dinner: Beef & Broccoli

Day 12

Breakfast: Breakfast Sausage
Lunch: Fish Stew
Dinner: Balsamic Chicken

Day 13

Breakfast: Spicy Breakfast Casserole
Lunch: Barbecue Pulled Pork
Dinner: Tikka Masala

Day 14

Breakfast: Breakfast Bake
Lunch: Squash & Zucchini
Dinner: Meatballs

Day 15

Breakfast: Sausage & Broccoli Breakfast Casserole
Lunch: Vegetarian Curry
Dinner: Crack Chicken

Day 16

Breakfast: Eggs, Leeks & Mushrooms
Lunch: Beef Stroganoff

Dinner: Shrimp Scampi

Day 17

Breakfast: Breakfast Frittata
Lunch: Salmon with Lemon Cream Sauce
Dinner: Chicken with Green Beans

Day 18

Breakfast: Breakfast Casserole
Lunch: Tuscan Garlic Chicken
Dinner: Pork Curry

Day 19

Breakfast: Bacon & Egg Breakfast
Lunch: Stewed Veggies
Dinner: Greek Chicken

Day 20

Breakfast: Breakfast Bake
Lunch: Beef Stroganoff
Dinner: Cheesy Broccoli Quiche

Day 21

Breakfast: Sausage & Broccoli Breakfast Casserole
Lunch: Chicken Fajitas
Dinner: Spicy Pork Chops

Day 22

Breakfast: Cauliflower Hash Browns
Lunch: Fish Stew
Dinner: Lamb Shanks with Green Beans

Day 23

Breakfast: Breakfast Sausage
Lunch: Carnitas
Dinner: Seafood Bisque

Day 24

Breakfast: Ham & Egg Casserole
Lunch: Stuffed Taco Peppers

Dinner: Shrimp & Sausage Gumbo

Day 25

Breakfast: Eggs, Leeks & Mushrooms
Lunch: Pork Roast with Creamy Gravy
Dinner: Greek Chicken

Day 26

Breakfast: Bacon & Egg Breakfast
Lunch: Tikka Masala
Dinner: Cauliflower Pizza

Day 27

Breakfast: Hash Brown & Turkey Bacon Casserole
Lunch: Crack Chicken
Dinner: Pulled Pork

Day 28

Breakfast: Egg, Tomato, Basil and Goat Cheese Omelet.
Lunch: Beef Curry
Dinner: Salmon with Lemon & Dill

Day 29

Breakfast: Breakfast Frittata
Lunch: Greek Chicken
Dinner: Vegetarian Curry

Day 30

Breakfast: Eggs, Leeks & Mushrooms
Lunch: Salmon with Lemon Cream Sauce
Dinner: Beef & Broccoli

CHAPTER 2: BREAKFAST AND BRUNCH

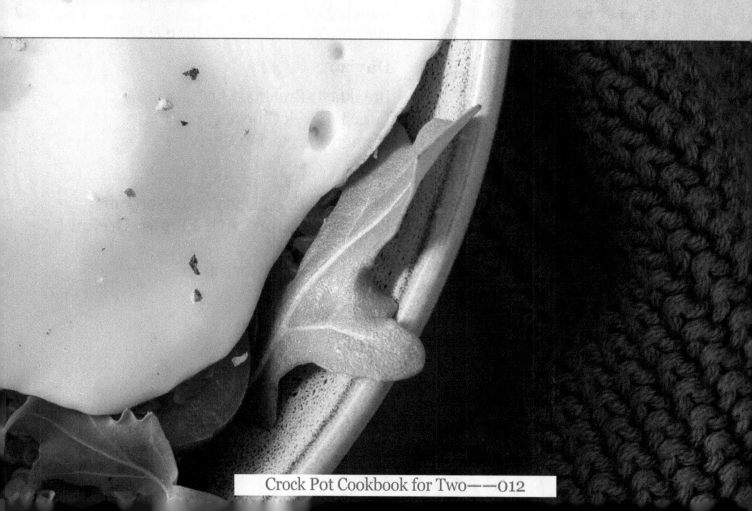

Ham Frittata

Preparation Time: 10 minutes
Cooking Time: 3 hours
Serves: 2

Ingredients:

- 6 cups of keto bread, cubed
- 4 oz. green chilies, diced
- 2 cups of almond milk
- 5 eggs, room temperature
- 1 tablespoon of mustard
- 10 oz. ham, cubed
- 4 oz. cheddar cheese, shredded
- Salt and black pepper- to taste
- Cooking spray

Method:

1.Start by greasing the base of your Crockpot.
2.Whisk the egg with all other Ingredients: and pour into crockpot.
3.Cover your crockpot and select the Low settings for 3 hours.
4.Remove the crockpot's lid.
5.Slice and serve warm.

Cheesy Cauliflower Garlic Bread

Preparation Time: 10 minutes
Cooking Time: 3 hours
Serves: 2

Ingredients:

- 12 oz. cauliflower florets, diced
- 2 large eggs
- 2 cups of mozzarella, shredded
- 3 tablespoons of coconut flour
- 1/2 teaspoon of salt
- 1/2 teaspoon of pepper
- 2 cloves garlic, minced
- 1/4 cup of fresh basil diced

Method:

1. Start by greasing the base of your Crockpot.
2. Mix and whisk all the Ingredients: together in a bowl except 1 cup of cheese
3. Pour this mixture into the pot and top with reserved these
4. Cover your crockpot and select the Low settings for 3 hours.
5. Remove the crockpot's lid.
6. Serve warm.

Bell Pepper Hash

Preparation Time: 10 minutes
Cooking Time: 3 hours
Serves: 2

Ingredients:

- 2 tablespoon of olive oil
- 3 eggplant, cubed
- 1 yellow onion, diced
- 1 red bell pepper, diced
- 1 teaspoon of garlic powder
- 1 teaspoon of sweet paprika
- 1 teaspoon of onion powder
- Salt and black pepper- to taste
- ½ cup of vegetable stock

Method:

1.Start by throwing all the Ingredients: into the Crockpot.
2.Cover your Crockpot and select the high settings for 3 hours.
3.Remove the crockpot's lid.
4.Check if the eggplants are al dente else cook for another 30 minutes or more.
5.Mix gently and serve warm.

Ham & Egg Casserole

Preparation Time: 10 minutes
Cooking Time: 1 hour and 30 minutes
Serves: 2

Ingredients:

• Cooking spray
• 1 tablespoon butter
• 1 lb. ham, sliced into cubes
• 2 stalks green onion, chopped
• 6 eggs
• ½ cup heavy cream
• 1 cup cheese, shredded
• Salt and pepper to taste

Method:

1.Spray the bottom of the slow cooker with oil.
2.Add the butter.
3.Stir in the green onions and ham.
4.In a bowl, beat the eggs and mix with the cream.
5.Pour the egg mixture over the ham and green onions.
6.Sprinkle cheese on top.
7.Season with salt and pepper.
8.Cook on high for 1 hour.
9.Stir and cook on high for an additional 30 minutes.

Breakfast Sausage

Preparation Time: 10 minutes
Cooking Time: 3 hours and 10 minutes
Serves: 2

Ingredients:

- 1 lb. pork sausage
- 1 teaspoon dried sage
- 1 teaspoon dried thyme
- ½ teaspoon garlic powder
- Salt and pepper to taste
- ½ cup red bell pepper, chopped
- ½ cup green bell pepper, chopped
- ½ cup onion, chopped
- 1 tablespoon ghee
- 12 eggs
- ½ cup coconut milk
- 1 tablespoon nutritional yeast

Method:

1. Put a skillet over medium heat.
2. Let it heat for 2 minutes.
3. Cook the pork sausage for 3 minutes, breaking it into small pieces.
4. Season with the dried herbs, spices, salt and pepper.
5. Cook for another 5 minutes.
6. Add the bell peppers and onion.
7. Brush the pot with the ghee and pour in the pork and veggie mixture.
8. In a bowl, mix the rest of the ingredients.
9. Pour the mixture into the pot.
10. Cover the pot.
11. Cook on low for 3 hours.

Breakfast Bake

Preparation Time: 15 minutes
Cooking Time: 2 hours
Serves: 2

Ingredients:

- 10 strips bacon
- ½ cup onion, chopped
- ½ cup sweet red pepper, chopped
- 2 lb. ground sausage
- 12 eggs
- ½ cup heavy cream
- Salt and pepper to taste
- 4 cups cheddar cheese

Method:

1. In a pan over medium heat, cook the bacon until golden and crispy.
2. Chop into bits and then set aside.
3. Add the onion and red peppers to the pan.
4. Cook for 3 minutes.
5. Add the sausage and cook until brown.
6. Beat the eggs in a bowl.
7. Add the heavy cream to the eggs and season with salt and pepper.
8. Add the sausage mixture to your slow cooker.
9. Sprinkle cheese and bacon on top of the sausage mixture.
10. Pour egg mixture on the topmost layer.
11. Cover the pot and cook on high for 2 hours.

Bacon & Egg Breakfast

Preparation Time: 15 minutes
Cooking Time: 1 hour and 5 minutes
Serves: 2

Ingredients:

- 10 slices bacon, cooked and chopped
- 10 eggs, beaten
- 1 cup whipping cream
- 8 oz. cheddar
- Salt and pepper to taste
- 1 tablespoon butter
- 3 stalks green onion, chopped

Method:

1. Cook the bacon in a pan over medium heat.
2. Drain and chop the bacon.
3. In a bowl, beat the eggs and stir in the cream and cheese.
4. Season with salt and pepper.
5. Add the butter to the slow cooker.
6. Pour the egg mixture into the pot.
7. Sprinkle bacon on top.
8. Cover the pot.
9. Cook on high for 1 hour.
10. Sprinkle green onions on top before serving.

Cauliflower Hash Browns

Preparation Time: 15 minutes
Cooking Time: 6 hours
Serves: 2

Ingredients:

• Cooking spray
• 12 eggs
• ½ cup milk
• Salt and pepper to taste
• ½ teaspoon dry mustard
• 1 head cauliflower, shredded
• 1 onion, diced
• 10 oz. precooked breakfast turkey sausage
• 2 cups cheddar cheese, shredded

Method:

1. Spray your slow cooker with oil.
2. Beat the eggs in a bowl.
3. Stir in the milk, salt, pepper and dry mustard.
4. Put 1/3 of the cauliflower in the bottom of the slow cooker.
5. Top with the 1/3 of the onion, 1/3 of the sausage and 1/3 of the cheese.
6. Repeat layers twice with the remaining ingredients.
7. Pour the egg and milk mixture over the layers.
8. Cook on low for 6 hours.

Garlic Sausage with Egg & Broccoli Bake

Preparation Time: 15 minutes
Cooking Time: 2 hours and 5 minutes
Serves: 2

Ingredients:

• 6 cloves garlic, crushed and minced
• 1 lb. breakfast turkey sausage
• 3 cups broccoli florets, blanched
• 12 eggs
• ½ cup heavy cream
• 2 cups cheddar cheese
• 2 tablespoons fresh parsley, chopped
• Salt and pepper to taste

Method:

1.In a pan over medium heat, cook the garlic for 1 minute.
2.Add the sausage and cook for 10 minutes.
3.In your slow cooker, add the broccoli florets in the bottom most layer.
4.Add the sausage on top.
5.In a bowl, beat the eggs and stir in the rest of the ingredients.
6.Pour the egg mixture on top of the layers.
7.Cover the pot.
8.Cook on high for 2 hours.

Breakfast Casserole

Preparation Time: 10 minutes
Cooking Time: 7 hours
Serves: 2

Ingredients:

- 12 eggs
- ¾ cup milk
- Salt to taste
- ¾ teaspoon ground paprika
- 1 tsp. dried oregano
- Cooking spray
- 2 ½ cups cauliflower, blanched
- 1 red bell pepper, chopped
- 1 lb. sausage slices, cooked
- 1 ½ cup cheddar cheese, grated

Method:

1. Combine the eggs and milk.
2. Season with the salt, paprika and oregano.
3. Spray the bottom of the pot with oil.
4. Alternate the layers of the ingredients with the cauliflowers at the bottom most of the pot topped with the red bell pepper, sausage and cheese.
5. Pour the egg mixture on top most layer.
6. Cover the pot and cook on low for 7 hours.

Hash brown & Turkey Bacon Casserole

Preparation Time: 20 minutes
Cooking Time: 4 hours and 5 minutes
Serves: 2

Ingredients:

• Cooking spray
• 1 package frozen hash browns
• 12 slices turkey bacon
• 1 red bell pepper, diced
• 1 red bell pepper, diced
• 16 eggs
• Salt and pepper to taste
• 1 cup cheddar cheese, grated

Method:

1. In a pan over medium high heat, cook the turkey bacon until golden and crispy. Set aside.
2. Spray your slow cooker with oil.
3. Arrange in even layers the hash browns, bacon, onion and bell peppers.
4. In a bowl, beat the eggs and season with salt and pepper.
5. Pour the egg mixture over the layers.
6. Sprinkle the cheese on top.
7. Cook on high for 4 hours.

Sweet Potato Breakfast Casserole

Preparation Time: 20 minutes
Cooking Time: 8 hours and 10 minutes
Serves: 2

Ingredients:

• 1 tablespoon butter
• 4 sausage, crumbled
• 2 cups sweet potatoes, grated
• 1 onion, diced
• 2 garlic cloves, crushed and minced
• 8 mushrooms, sliced
• 1 red bell pepper, diced
• 12 eggs
• 1 cup coconut milk
• Salt and pepper to taste
• 1 green onion, sliced

Method:

1. Melt butter in a pan over medium heat.
2. Add onion and garlic. Cook for 2 minutes.
3. Add sausage and cook for 5 minutes.
4. Arrange sweet potato shreds on the bottom of the slow cooker.
5. Pour the onion and sausage mixture on top.
6. Arrange the mushrooms and bell pepper on top of the onion and sausage.
7. In a bowl, mix the eggs and coconut milk.
8. Stir in the salt and pepper.
9. Pour this mixture on top of the layers.
10. Cook on low for 8 hours.
11. Garnish with the green onion.

Zucchini Bread

Preparation Time: 10 minutes
Cooking Time: 3 hours
Serves: 2

Ingredients:

- 1 cup of almond flour
- 1/3 cup of coconut flour
- 2 teaspoons of cinnamon
- 1 1/2 teaspoon of baking powder
- 1/2 teaspoon of baking soda
- 1/2 teaspoon of salt
- 1/2 teaspoon of xanthan gum optional
- 3 eggs
- 1/3 cup of coconut oil softened, or butter
- 1/2 cup of swerve
- 2 teaspoons of vanilla
- 2 cups of zucchini, shredded
- 1/2 cup of walnuts or pecans, diced

Method:

1. Start by beating all the wet Ingredients: in an electric mixer.
2. Whisk the dry Ingredients: separately in a bowl.
3. Add this flour mixture to the prepared wet mixture and beat well until smooth.
4. Fold in walnut and shredded zucchini, then mix roughly.
5. Spread this zucchini batter into a greased loaf pan (suitable to the size of the crockpot)
6. Place this pan in the crockpot.
7. Cover your Crockpot and select the high settings for 3 hours.
8. Remove the crockpot's lid.
9. Slice and serve warm.

Bacon, Egg & Kale Casserole

Preparation Time: 15 minutes
Cooking Time: 1 hour and 40 minutes
Serves: 2

Ingredients:

- 3 bacon slices
- 3 tablespoons shallots, chopped
- 1 cup mushrooms, chopped
- ½ cup red bell pepper, chopped
- 9 leaves kale, shredded
- 6 eggs
- Salt and pepper to taste
- 1 tablespoon butter
- 1 cup Parmesan cheese, grated

Method:

1. Cook bacon in a pan until golden and crispy.
2. Add the shallots, mushrooms and red bell pepper.
3. Sauté for 1 to 2 minutes.
4. Stir in the kale and remove from heat.
5. In a bowl, mix the eggs, salt and pepper.
6. Put your slow cooker over high heat and put the butter inside.
7. Once the butter has melted, add the vegetables.
8. Pour the egg mixture into the pot.
9. Sprinkle with the cheese on top.
10. Cook on high for 1 hour and 30 minutes.

CHAPTER 3: SOUPS AND STEWS

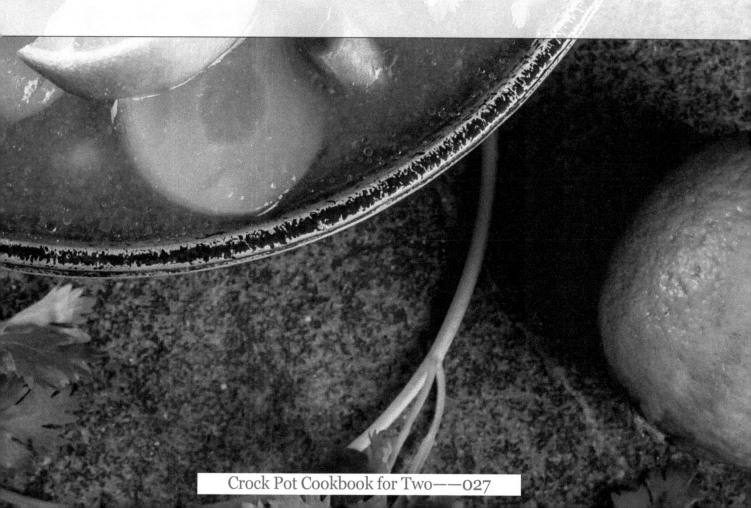

Chicken Taco Soup

Preparation Time: 15 minutes
Cooking Time: 7 hours
Serves: 2

Ingredients:

• 1 onion, chopped
• 15 oz. canned corn kernels
• 15 oz. canned black beans
• 16 oz. canned chili beans
• 10 oz. canned diced tomatoes
• 8 oz. tomato sauce
• 1 packet taco seasoning
• 3 chicken breast fillets
• 8 oz. cheddar cheese, shredded
• Crushed tortilla chips

Method:

1. Add all the ingredients except chicken breast, cheese and tortilla chips in your slow cooker.
2. Mix well.
3. Arrange the chicken breast fillets on top of the mixture.
4. Cover the pot.
5. Cook on low for 5 hours.
6. Take the chicken out of the pot and shred.
7. Put the shredded chicken back to the pot.
8. Cook on low for 2 hours.
Sprinkle cheese and garnish with tortilla chips before serving.

Creamy Lemon Chicken Kale Soup

Preparation Time: 10 minutes
Cooking Time: 6 hours
Serves: 2

Ingredients:

- 4 cups of shredded chicken
- 6 cups of bone broth
- 1 bunch of kale, rinsed, drained and sliced into 1/2-inch strips
- 3 lemons
- 2 tablespoons of fresh lemon juice
- 1 cup of onions, diced
- 1/2 cup of olive oil
- salt to taste

Method:

1. Start by throwing all the Ingredients: into your Crockpot.
2. Mix well and cover the Crockpot with its lid.
3. Select the Low settings for 6 hours.
4. Serve warm.

Bacon & Chicken Chowder

Preparation Time: 30 minutes
Cooking Time: 7 hours and 15 minutes
Serves: 2

Ingredients:

- 4 tablespoons butter, divided
- 1 onion, sliced thinly
- 1 shallot, chopped
- 4 cloves garlic, crushed and minced
- 1 leek, trimmed and sliced
- 2 ribs celery, chopped
- 6 oz. mushrooms, sliced
- 2 cups chicken stock, divided
- 1 lb. chicken breasts
- 8 oz. cream cheese
- 1 cup heavy cream
- 1 lb. bacon, cooked crisp and crumbled
- Salt and pepper to taste
- 1 teaspoon garlic powder
- 1 teaspoon dried thyme

Method:

1.Add half of the butter to the slow cooker.
2.Add the onion, shallot, garlic, leek, mushroom and celery to the pot.
3.Pour in half of the stock.
4.Season with salt and pepper.
5.Cover the pot.
6.Cook on low for 1 hour.
7.While waiting, cook the chicken in butter in a pan over medium heat.
8.Cook until brown on both sides.
9.Slice into cubes and set aside.
10.Add the rest of the ingredients except the bacon to the pot.
11.Stir well.
12.Add the chicken cubes and bacon.
13.Cover the pot and cook on low for 6 hours.

White Chicken Chili Soup

Preparation Time: 10 minutes
Cooking Time: 4 hours
Serves: 2

Ingredients:

- 2 lbs. boneless, skinless chicken breasts
- 2 onions, diced
- 4 cups of chicken broth
- 1 teaspoon of coriander powder
- 4 stalks celery, diced
- 1 tablespoon of salt
- 1 2 jalapeño pepper, minced
- 10 cloves garlic, smashed
- 1 tablespoon of chili powder
- 1 teaspoon of cumin
- 1 teaspoon of oregano
- ½ teaspoon of black pepper
- Serve with cilantro

Method:

1.Start by throwing all the Ingredients: into your Crockpot.
2.Mix well and cover the Crockpot with its lid.
3.Select the High settings for 4 hours.
4.Serve warm.

Taco Soup

Preparation Time: 15 minutes
Cooking Time: 4 hours
Serves: 2

Ingredients:

- 1 tablespoon butter
- 2 lb. ground beef
- 2 cloves garlic, crushed and minced
- ½ cup onion, diced
- 2 tablespoons homemade taco seasoning
- ½ teaspoon ancho chili powder
- 20 oz. canned Rotel with green peppers
- 8 oz. cream cheese
- ½ cup cilantro, chopped
- 4 cups beef broth

Method:

1. In a pan over medium heat, cook the onion and garlic for 2 minutes.
2. Add the ground beef and cook until brown.
3. Transfer the ground mixture to your slow cooker.
4. Stir in the rest of the ingredients.
5. Seal the pot.
6. Cook on low for 4 hours.

Mexican Chicken Soup

Preparation Time: 15 minutes
Cooking Time: 4 hours
Serves: 2

Ingredients:

- 2 teaspoons oil
- 1 onion, chopped
- 1 tablespoon garlic, crushed and minced
- 4 chicken breast fillets
- 14 oz. canned roasted tomatoes
- 1 red bell pepper, chopped
- 1 ½ teaspoons cumin
- 1 teaspoon dried oregano
- 1 ½ teaspoon chipotle chili powder
- 1 ½ chicken stock
- 1 cup half and half
- ½ cup cream cheese
- 1 cup Mexican blend cheese
- Salt to taste
- Cilantro

Method:

1. Pour the oil into a pan over medium heat.
2. Add the onion and garlic. Cook for 2 minutes.
3. In the slow cooker, add the chicken breast fillet, tomatoes, onion, garlic, spices, chicken stock and salt.
4. Seal the pot.
5. Cook on high for 3 hours.
6. Add the rest of the ingredients except cilantro and cook on high for 20 minutes.
7. Take the chicken out and shred using 2 forks.
8. Put the shredded chicken back to the pot.
9. Garnish with cilantro before serving.

Chicken Cordon Bleu Soup

Preparation Time: 10 minutes
Cooking Time: 6 hours
Serves: 2

Ingredients:

• 6 cups of chicken stock
• 12 oz. diced ham
• 5 oz. mushrooms, diced
• 4 oz. onion, diced
• 2 teaspoons of dried tarragon
• 1 teaspoon of salt, more to taste
• 1 teaspoon of black pepper
• 1 lb. chicken breast, cubed
• 4 cloves garlic, minced
• 3 tablespoons of salted butter
• 1 1/2 cups of heavy cream
• 1/2 cup of sour cream
• 1/2 cup of grated Parmesan cheese
• 4 oz. Swiss cheese

Method:

1.Start by throwing all the Ingredients: into your Crockpot.
2.Mix well and cover the Crockpot with its lid.
3.Select the Low settings for 6 hours.
4.Serve warm.

Buffalo Chicken Soup

Preparation Time: 10 minutes
Cooking Time: 4 hours and 10 minutes
Serves: 2

Ingredients:

- ½ tablespoon ghee
- ¼ cup onion, diced
- ¾ cup celery, sliced thinly
- 2 cups chicken broth
- ½ cup coconut milk
- ½ cup ranch dressing
- ¼ cup hot sauce
- Salt to taste
- ¼ teaspoon paprika
- ½ lb. chicken thighs
- 1 tablespoon tapioca starch
- Green onion, chopped

Method:

1. Add the ghee to a pan over medium heat.
2. Add the onion and celery.
3. Cook for 3 minutes.
4. Transfer to your slow cooker.
5. Add the rest of the ingredients except tapioca starch and green onion.
6. Stir well.
7. Cover the pot and cook on high for 3 hours.
8. In a bowl, mix the tapioca starch with 2 tablespoons cooking liquid.
9. Stir into the pot.
10. Cook for another 2 hours.
11. Shred the chicken and put it back to the pot.
12. Garnish with the green onions.

Mexican Chicken Low Carb Soup

Preparation Time: 10 minutes
Cooking Time: 4 hours
Serves: 2

Ingredients:

- 1 1/2 lbs. chicken pieces boneless/skinless
- 15.5 oz. chunky salsa
- 15 oz. chicken broth
- 8 oz. Monterey, shredded

Method:

1. Start by throwing all the Ingredients: into your Crockpot.
2. Mix well and cover the Crockpot with its lid.
3. Select the High settings for 4 hours.
4. Serve warm.

Beef & Vegetable Soup

Preparation Time: 25 minutes
Cooking Time: 6 hours and 10 minutes
Serves: 2

Ingredients:

- 1 teaspoon butter
- 2 lb. stew meat, cubed
- 2 tablespoons red wine vinegar
- 32 oz. reduced-sodium beef broth
- 1 onion, chopped
- ¼ cup green beans, sliced
- 6 oz. celeriac, diced
- ¼ cup carrot, diced
- 2 tablespoons tomato paste
- 28 oz. canned diced tomatoes
- 2 cloves garlic, crushed
- 1/2 teaspoon dried rosemary
- 1/2 teaspoon dried thyme
- Salt and pepper to taste
- 4 slices bacon, chopped and cooked

Method:

1. Add the butter to a pan over medium heat.
2. Cook the beef cubes until brown.
3. Season with salt and pepper. Set aside.
4. Reduce heat to medium low.
5. Transfer the liquid mixture to the slow cooker with the remaining broth.
6. Add the beef and the rest of the ingredients to the pot.
7. Mix well.
8. Cover the pot.
9. Cook on low for 6 hours.
10. Sprinkle bacon bits on top before serving.

Zucchini Soup

Preparation Time: 20 minutes
Cooking Time: 4 hours and 10 minutes
Serves: 2

Ingredients:

- Cooking spray
- 1 ½ lb. Italian sausage
- 2 cups celery, chopped
- 2 lb. zucchini, sliced
- 56 oz. canned diced tomatoes
- 1 red bell pepper, sliced
- 1 green bell pepper, sliced
- 1 cup onion, chopped
- Salt to taste
- 1 teaspoon white sugar
- 1 teaspoon dried oregano
- 1 teaspoon Italian seasoning
- 1 teaspoon dried basil
- ¼ teaspoon garlic powder
- 5 tablespoons Parmesan cheese, grated

Method:

1. Spray your pan with oil.
2. Cook the sausage until brown. Drain the fat.
3. Add the celery and cook for 10 minutes. Set aside.
4. Put the sausage mixture along with the rest of the ingredients except Parmesan cheese in your slow cooker.
5. Cover the pot.
6. Cook on low for 4 hours.
7. Sprinkle Parmesan cheese on top before serving.

Broccoli & Cheese Soup

Preparation Time: 10 minutes
Cooking Time: 3 hours
Serves: 2

Ingredients:

- 2 cups water
- 2 cups chicken broth
- 2 tablespoons butter
- 8 oz. cream cheese
- 1 cup whipping cream
- ½ cup Parmesan cheese
- 5 cups broccoli florets
- 2 ½ cups cheddar cheese, shredded
- Salt and pepper to taste

Method:

1. Pour the water and broth into your slow cooker.
2. Stir in the butter, cream cheese and cream.
3. Add the Parmesan cheese and broccoli.
4. Cover the pot.
5. Cook on low for 3 hours.
6. Top with the cheddar and season with salt and pepper before serving.

Cheesy Cauliflower Soup

Preparation Time: 15 minutes
Cooking Time: 4 hours and 15 minutes
Serves: 2

Ingredients:

- 1 onion, chopped
- 6 cups cauliflower florets
- 2 cups water
- 1 cup chicken broth
- 2 cups almond milk
- 2 scoops protein bone broth flakes
- 1 teaspoon Dijon mustard
- 8 oz. cheddar cheese, shredded

Method:

1. Put the onion, cauliflower, water, broth, almond milk and bone broth flakes into your slow cooker.
2. Mix well.
3. Cover the pot.
4. Cook on low for 3 hours.
5. Transfer the contents to an immersion blender.
6. Pulse until smooth.
7. Put the mixture back to the pot.
8. Stir in mustard and cheese.
9. Cook until the cheese has melted.

No Noodle Chicken Soup

Preparation Time: 10 minutes
Cooking Time: 8 hours
Serves: 2

Ingredients:

- 1 whole chicken
- 2 bunches celery, diced into 4-inch pieces
- 3 tablespoons of salt
- 1 teaspoon of black pepper
- 6 cups of water
- 4 cups of mixed frozen vegetables

Method:

1.Start by throwing all the Ingredients: into your Crockpot.
2.Mix well and cover the Crockpot with its lid.
3.Select the Low settings for 8 hours.
4.Serve warm.

CHAPTER 4: VEGETABLES AND VEGETARIAN

Squash & Zucchini

Preparation Time: 5 minutes
Cooking Time: 6 hours
Serves: 2

Ingredients:

- 2 cups zucchini, sliced
- 2 cups yellow squash, sliced
- ½ teaspoon salt
- ¼ teaspoon pepper
- 1 teaspoon garlic powder
- 1 teaspoon Italian seasoning
- ¼ cup butter, sliced into cubes
- ¼ cup Parmesan cheese, grated

Method:

1. Put zucchini and squash in a slow cooker.
2. Season with the salt, pepper, garlic powder and Italian seasoning.
3. Top with the butter and cheese.
4. Cover the pot.
5. Cook on low for 5 hours.

Rich Cheesy Broccoli Soup

Preparation Time: 10 minutes
Cooking Time: 5 hours
Serves: 2

Ingredients:

- 1 tablespoon of olive oil
- 2 tablespoons of butter
- 2 medium carrots, peeled and diced
- 1 small yellow onion, diced
- 2 tablespoons of almond flour
- 1 garlic clove, minced
- 3 cups of homemade vegetable broth
- 5 cups of broccoli florets
- 1 teaspoon of dill weed
- 1 teaspoon of smoked paprika
- Salt and black pepper, to taste
- 4 American cheese slices, cut into pieces
- 1 cup of Colby Jack cheese, shredded
- 1 cup of Pepper Jack cheese, shredded
- ½ cup of Parmesan cheese, shredded

Method:

1. Start by throwing all the Ingredients: into your Crockpot.
2. Cover its lid and cook for 5 hours on Low setting.
3. Once done, remove its lid and give it a stir.
4. Garnish as desired.
5. Serve warm.

Stuffed Taco Peppers

Preparation Time: 15 minutes
Cooking Time: 4 hours
Serves: 2

Ingredients:

- 1 cup cauliflower rice
- 4 cups ground turkey
- 1 cup Monterey Jack cheese, shredded
- ½ teaspoon onion powder
- ½ teaspoon garlic powder
- 1 teaspoon chili powder
- 1 ½ tablespoons olive oil
- 6 red bell peppers, tops sliced off and seeded
- 1 cup water

Method:

1. In a large bowl, combine all the ingredients except the bell peppers and water.
2. Stuff each red bell pepper shell with the mixture.
3. Arrange these into your slow cooker.
4. Pour the water into your pot.
5. Cover the pot and cook on high for 4 hours.

Carrots with Mushroom Sauce

Preparation Time: 10 minutes
Cooking Time: 4 hours
Serves: 2

Ingredients:

- 2 tablespoons of butter
- 2 garlic cloves, minced
- 1 tablespoon of fresh sage leaves, diced
- 1 lb. fresh mushrooms, sliced
- Salt and black pepper, to taste
- ¼ cup of heavy cream
- 1 scallion, diced
- 3 large carrots, spiralized with blade C
- 1 cup of whipping cream

Method:

1.Start by throwing all the Ingredients: into your Crockpot.
2.Cover its lid and cook for 4 hours on Low setting.
3.Once done, remove its lid and give it a stir.
4.Garnish as desired.
5.Serve warm.

Vegetarian Curry

Preparation Time: 15 minutes
Cooking Time: 4 hours
Serves: 2

Ingredients:

- 3 cups coconut milk
- 2 tablespoons curry powder
- Salt to taste
- 1 teaspoon red pepper flakes, crushed
- 1 ½ teaspoons granulated garlic
- 6 cups pineapple chunks
- 1 lb. sweet potatoes, sliced
- 2 green bell peppers, sliced
- 2 onions, sliced

Method:

1. Combine all the ingredients in your slow cooker.
2. Mix well.
3. Cover the pot.
4. Cook on high for 4 hours.

Stewed Veggies

Preparation Time: 20 minutes
Cooking Time: 4 hours and 16 minutes
Serves: 2

Ingredients:

• Olive oil
• 1 onion, chopped
• 1 red bell pepper, chopped
• 1 green bell pepper, chopped
• 2 cloves garlic, minced
• 2 cups vegetable broth
• 14 oz. canned diced tomatoes
• 15 oz. chickpeas, rinsed and drained
• 1 tablespoon curry powder
• 1 tablespoon maple syrup
• 1 tablespoon ginger, chopped
• Salt and pepper to taste
• 1 head cauliflower, sliced into florets
• 10 oz. baby spinach, chopped
• 1 cup coconut milk

Method:

1.Pour the oil into a pan over medium high heat.
2.Cook the onion and bell peppers for 5 minutes.
3.Add the garlic and cook for 1 minute.
4.Pour the mixture into your slow cooker.
5.Add the rest of the ingredients except the cauliflower, spinach and coconut milk.
6.Cover and cook on high for 3 hours.
7.Stir in the cauliflower. Cover and cook on high 1 hour.
8.Stir in the coconut milk and spinach. Cook on high for 10 minutes.

Spinach with Tomato Sauce

Preparation Time: 10 minutes
Cooking Time: 3
Serves: 2

Ingredients:

- 2 tablespoons of olive oil
- 1 medium onion, diced
- 1 tablespoon of garlic, minced
- ½ teaspoon of red pepper flakes, crushed
- 8 cups of fresh spinach, chopped
- 1 cup of tomatoes, diced
- ½ cup of homemade tomato puree
- ½ cup of white wine
- ¾ cup of vegetable broth
- ½ cup of cream cheese

Method:

1. Start by throwing all the Ingredients: into your Crockpot except cream cheese.
2. Cover its lid and cook for 3 hours on Low setting.
3. Once done, remove its lid and give it a stir.
4. Stir in cream cheese and mix gently.
5. Garnish as desired.
6. Serve warm.

Tomato Soup

Preparation Time: 10 minutes
Cooking Time: 2 hours
Serves: 2

Ingredients:

- ½ tablespoon of olive oil
- 1 small onion, diced
- 1 garlic clove, minced
- 1 ½ lb. tomatoes, diced
- 1 tablespoon of sugar-free tomato sauce
- 1 teaspoon of parsley, dried, crushed
- 1 teaspoon of dried basil, crushed
- Black pepper, to taste
- 2 cups of vegetable broth
- 2 tablespoons of Erythritol
- ½ tablespoon of balsamic vinegar
- ¼ cup of fresh basil, diced

Method:

1. Start by throwing all the Ingredients: into your Crockpot.
2. Cover its lid and cook for 2 hours on High setting.
3. Once done, remove its lid and give it a stir.
4. Garnish as desired.
5. Serve warm.

Zucchini Lasagna

Preparation Time: 45 minutes
Cooking Time: 4 hours and 45 minutes
Serves: 2

Ingredients:

- 4 cups zucchinis, sliced into thin strips
- 1 tablespoon salt
- 2 tablespoons coconut oil
- 1 cup onion, diced
- 1 tablespoon garlic, minced
- ½ tablespoon ginger, minced
- 1 lb. ground turkey
- Pepper to taste
- 1 cup coconut milk
- ¼ cup low sodium soy sauce
- ¼ cup creamy peanut butter
- 1 tablespoon rice vinegar
- 2 tablespoons coconut sugar
- 2 tablespoons hot sauce
- 1 tablespoon fish sauce
- 1 tablespoon freshly squeezed lime juice
- 15 oz. ricotta cheese
- 1 egg
- ½ cup cilantro, chopped
- 2 cups Napa cabbage, chopped
- ½ cup water chestnuts, diced
- 8 oz. mozzarella cheese

Method:

1.Preheat your oven to 350 degrees F.
2.Arrange the zucchini slices in a baking pan.
3.Sprinkle salt on top.
4.Bake in the oven for 20 minutes.
5.While waiting, pour the coconut oil in a pan over medium heat.
6.Add the onion, garlic, ginger and turkey.
7.Season with pepper.

8. Cook for 10 minutes.
9. Stir in the coconut milk, soy sauce, peanut butter, vinegar, sugar, hot sauce, fish sauce and lime juice.
10. Bring to a boil and then simmer for 4 minutes.
11. Take the zucchini strips out of the oven and press with a paper towel to get rid of extra moisture.
12. In a bowl, beat the egg and cheese. Set aside.
13. Spray your slow cooker with oil.
14. Spread half of the turkey mixture on the bottom part.
15. Layer the zucchini on top of the turkey.
16. Top with the ricotta.
17. Sprinkle half of the cilantro, cabbage, water chestnuts and Mozzarella cheese.
18. Repeat the layers.
19. Cover the pot and cook on low for 4 hours.

Tikka Masala

Preparation Time: 15 minutes
Cooking Time: 1 hour and 35 minutes
Serves: 2

Ingredients:

For the cauliflower:
- 1 head cauliflower, sliced into florets
- 1 tablespoon olive oil
- 1 teaspoon garam masala
- 1 teaspoon ground cumin
- ½ teaspoon cayenne pepper
- Salt to taste

For the sauce:
- 4 tablespoons butter
- 1 onion, diced
- 1 tablespoon ginger, minced
- 2 cloves garlic, minced
- 1 ½ teaspoon paprika
- 1 tablespoon garam masala
- ½ teaspoon cayenne pepper
- 1 ½ cups canned crushed tomatoes
- 1 teaspoon ground cumin
- ½ cup water
- ½ cup coconut cream
- Salt to taste
- ¼ cup cilantro, minced

Method:

1. Preheat your oven to 425 degrees F.
2. In a large bowl, toss the cauliflower florets in oil and spices under the cauliflower ingredients.
3. Put in a baking pan and bake for 30 minutes.
4. In your slow cooker over medium heat, melt the butter, and cook the onion, ginger and garlic for 5 minutes.
5. Stir in the rest of the ingredients except the cilantro.
6. Cover the pot and cook on high for 1 hour.
7. Garnish with the cilantro before serving.

Cheesy Broccoli Quiche

Preparation Time: 20 minutes
Cooking Time: 2 hours and 15 minutes
Serves: 2

Ingredients:

• Water
• 3 cups broccoli florets
• 9 eggs
• 8 oz. cream cheese
• ¼ teaspoon onion powder
• Salt and pepper to taste
• Cooking spray
• 2 cups cheddar cheese, divided

Method:

1. Fill your pot with water.
2. Place it over medium high heat and bring to a boil.
3. Once the water is boiling, add the broccoli florets.
4. Boil for 3 minutes.
5. Drain and rinse the broccoli under running water. Set aside.
6. In a bowl, beat the eggs and cream cheese.
7. Season with the onion powder, salt and pepper.
8. Spray your slow cooker with oil.
9. Arrange the broccoli in the bottom of the pot.
10. Sprinkle half of the cheddar cheese on top.
11. Pour the egg mixture on top.
12. Cover the pot.
13. Cook on high for 2 hours and 15 minutes.
14. Sprinkle remaining cheddar on top.
15. Let sit for 10 minutes before serving.

Nutty Brussels Sprout

Preparation Time: 10 minutes
Cooking Time: 3 hours
Serves: 2

Ingredients:

- 1 lb. Brussels sprouts, trimmed and halved
- ¼ cup of butter, melted
- ½ cup of almonds, diced
- ½ cup of vegetable stock

Method:

1.Start by throwing all the Ingredients: into your Crockpot.
2.Cover its lid and cook for 3 hours on Low setting.
3.Once done, remove its lid and give it a stir.
4.Garnish as desired.
5.Serve warm.

Pesto Peppers

Preparation Time: 10 minutes
Cooking Time: 4 hours
Serves: 2

Ingredients:

- 12 Baby bell peppers, cut into halves lengthwise
- 6 tablespoon of Jarred basil pesto
- 1 tablespoon of Lemon juice
- 1 tablespoon of Olive oil
- 1 lb. zucchini, sliced
- 1/4 teaspoon of Red pepper flakes, crushed
- Salt and black pepper- to taste
- Handful parsley, chopped
- ½ cup of vegetable stock

Method:

1. Start by throwing all the Ingredients: into your Crockpot.
2. Cover its lid and cook for 4 hours on Low setting.
3. Once done, remove its lid and give it a stir.
4. Garnish as desired.
5. Serve warm.

Cauliflower Pizza

Preparation Time: 15 minutes
Cooking Time: 3 hours
Serves: 2

Ingredients:

For the crust:
- 1 head cauliflower, chopped
- 2 eggs, beaten
- ½ cup Italian cheese blend, shredded
- 1 teaspoon dried Italian seasoning blend
- Salt to taste

For the toppings:
- ½ cup Alfredo sauce
- 1 ½ cups Italian cheese blend, shredded
- ½ teaspoon dried rosemary

Method:

1. Put the cauliflower in a food processor.
2. Pulse until consistency is similar to rice.
3. Transfer to a bowl and stir in the crust ingredients.
4. Spray oil on your slow cooker.
5. Press the mixture on the bottom part of the pot.
6. Spread Alfredo sauce on top.
7. Top with the cheese and rosemary.
8. Cover.
9. Cook on high for 3 hours.
10. Let sit for 30 minutes before slicing and serving.

CHAPTER 5: POULTRY

Balsamic Chicken

Preparation Time: 15 minutes
Cooking Time: 4 hours
Serves: 2

Ingredients:

- 1 tablespoon olive oil
- 6 chicken breasts fillets
- 30 oz. canned diced tomatoes
- 1 onion, sliced thinly
- 4 cloves garlic
- ½ cup balsamic vinegar
- 1 teaspoon dried rosemary
- 1 teaspoon dried basil
- 1 teaspoon dried oregano
- ½ teaspoon thyme
- Salt and pepper to taste

Method:

1. Add the oil to your slow cooker.
2. Place the chicken breasts inside the pot.
3. Put the onions on top with the garlic cloves and herbs.
4. Pour the vinegar and tomatoes on top.
5. Cover the pot and cook on high for 4 hours.

Turkey Meatballs

Preparation Time: 10 minutes
Cooking Time: 6 hours
Serves: 2

Ingredients:

- 1 lb. turkey meat, ground
- 1 yellow onion, minced
- 4 garlic cloves, minced
- ¼ cup of parsley, chopped
- salt, and black pepper to taste
- 1 teaspoon of oregano, dried
- 1 egg, whisked
- ¼ cup of almond milk
- 2 teaspoon of coconut aminos
- 12 mushrooms, diced
- 1 cup of chicken stock
- 2 tablespoon of olive oil
- 2 tablespoons of butter

Method:

1. Thoroughly mix turkey meat with onion, garlic, parsley, pepper, salt, egg, aminos, and oregano in a bowl.
2. Make 1-inch small meatballs out of this mixture.
3. Add these meatballs along with other Ingredients: into the Crockpot.
4. Cover it and cook for 6 hours on Low Settings.
5. Garnish as desired.
6. Serve warm.

Chicken with Green Beans

Preparation Time: 5 minutes
Cooking Time: 4 hours
Serves: 2

Ingredients:

• 1 onion, diced
• 2 cloves garlic, crushed and minced
• 2 tomatoes, diced
• ¼ cup dill, chopped
• 1 lb. green beans
• 1 cup chicken broth
• 1 tablespoon lemon juice
• 4 chicken thighs
• Salt and pepper to taste
• 2 tablespoons olive oil

Method:

1.Put the onion, garlic, tomatoes, dill and green beans in your slow cooker.
2.Pour in the chicken broth and lemon juice.
3.Season with salt and pepper.
4.Mix well.
5.Add the chicken on top of the vegetables.
6.Drizzle chicken with oil.
7.Cover the pot.
8.Cook on high for 4 hours.

Greek Chicken

Preparation Time: 15 minutes
Cooking Time: 2 hours
Serves: 2

Ingredients:

- 2 tablespoons olive oil
- 3 cloves garlic
- 2 lb. chicken thigh fillets
- Salt and pepper to taste
- 1 cup kalamata olives
- 8 oz. marinated artichoke hearts, rinsed and drained
- 12 oz. roasted red peppers, drained and sliced
- 1 onion, sliced
- ½ cup chicken broth
- ¼ cup red wine vinegar
- 1 tablespoon lemon juice
- 1 teaspoon dried oregano
- 1 teaspoon dried thyme
- 2 tablespoons arrowroot starch

Method:

1. Season the chicken with salt and pepper.
2. Put a pan over medium high heat.
3. Add the oil and garlic.
4. Cook for 1 minute, stirring frequently.
5. Add the chicken and cook for 2 minutes per side.
6. Transfer the chicken to the slow cooker.
7. Add the olives, artichoke hearts and peppers around the chicken.
8. Sprinkle onion on top.
9. In a bowl, mix the rest of the ingredients except the arrowroot starch.
10. Pour this into the slow cooker.
11. Cover the pot.
12. Cook on high for 2 hours.
13. Get 3 tablespoons of the cooking liquid.
14. Stir in the arrowroot starch to the liquid and put it back to the pot.
Simmer for 15 minutes before serving.

Ranch Chicken

Preparation Time: 5 minutes
Cooking Time: 4 hours and 5 minutes
Serves: 2

Ingredients:

- 2 lb. chicken breast fillet
- 3 tablespoons butter
- 4 oz. cream cheese
- 3 tablespoons ranch dressing mix

Method:

1. Add the chicken to your slow cooker.
2. Place the butter and cream cheese on top of the chicken.
3. Sprinkle ranch dressing mix.
4. Seal the pot.
5. Cook on high for 4 hours.
6. Shred the chicken using forks and serve.

Barbeque Chicken Wings

Preparation Time: 10 minutes
Cooking Time: 3 hours
Serves: 2

Ingredients:

- 2 lbs. chicken wings
- 1/2 cup of water
- 1/2 teaspoon of basil, dried
- 3/4 cup of BBQ sauce
- 1/2 cup of lime juice
- 1 teaspoon of red pepper, crushed
- 2 teaspoons of paprika
- 1/2 cup of swerve
- Salt and black pepper- to taste
- A pinch cayenne peppers

Method:

1. Start by throwing all the Ingredients: into the Crockpot and mix them well.
2. Cover it and cook for 3 hours on Low Settings.
3. Garnish as desired.
4. Serve warm.

Chicken Fajitas

Preparation Time: 10 minutes
Cooking Time: 3 hours
Serves: 2

Ingredients:

- 1 ½ lb. chicken breast fillet
- ½ cup salsa
- 8 oz. cream cheese
- 1 teaspoon cumin
- 1 teaspoon paprika
- Salt and pepper to taste
- 1 onion, sliced
- 1 clove garlic, minced
- 1 red bell pepper, sliced
- 1 green bell pepper, sliced
- 1 teaspoon lime juice

Method:

1. Combine all the ingredients except the lime wedges in your slow cooker.
2. Cover the pot.
3. Cook on high for 3 hours.
4. Shred the chicken.
5. Drizzle with lime juice.
6. Serve with toppings like sour cream and cheese.

Saucy Duck

Preparation Time: 10 minutes
Cooking Time: 6 hours
Serves: 2

Ingredients:

- 1 duck, cut into small chunks
- 4 garlic cloves, minced
- 4 tablespoons of swerves
- 2 green onions, roughly diced
- 4 tablespoon of soy sauce
- 4 tablespoon of sherry wine
- 1/4 cup of water
- 1-inch ginger root, sliced
- A pinch salt
- black pepper to taste

Method:

1.Start by throwing all the Ingredients: into the Crockpot and mix them well.
2.Cover it and cook for 6 hours on Low Settings.
3.Garnish as desired.
4.Serve warm.

Sesame Ginger Chicken

Preparation Time: 5 minutes
Cooking Time: 5 hours
Serves: 2

Ingredients:

- 1 ½ lb. chicken breast fillet
- ½ cup tomato sauce
- ¼ cup low-sugar peach jam
- ¼ cup chicken broth
- 2 tablespoons coconut aminos
- 1 ½ tablespoons sesame oil
- 1 tablespoon honey
- 1 teaspoon ground ginger
- 2 cloves garlic, minced
- ¼ cup onion, minced
- ¼ teaspoon red pepper flakes, crushed
- 2 tablespoons red bell pepper, chopped
- 1 ½ tablespoons green onion, chopped
- 2 teaspoons sesame seeds

Method:

1. Combine all the ingredients except green onion and sesame seeds in your slow cooker.
2. Mix well.
3. Cover the pot and cook on high for 4 hours.
4. Garnish with the green onion and sesame seeds.

Chicken Roux Gumbo

Preparation Time: 10 minutes
Cooking Time: 6 hours
Serves: 2

Ingredients:

- 1 lb. chicken thighs, cut into halves
- 1 tablespoon of vegetable oil
- 1 lb smoky sausage, sliced, crispy, and crumbled.
- Salt and black pepper- to taste
Aromatics:
- 1 bell pepper, diced
- 2 quarts' chicken stock
- 15 oz. canned tomatoes, diced
- 1 celery stalk, diced
- salt to taste
- 4 garlic cloves, minced
- 1/2 lbs. okra, sliced
- 1 yellow onion, diced
- a dash tabasco sauce
For the roux:
- 1/2 cup of almond flour
- 1/4 cup of vegetable oil
- 1 teaspoon of Cajun spice

Method:

1. Start by throwing all the Ingredients: except okra and roux Ingredients: into the Crockpot.
2. Cover it and cook for 5 hours on Low Settings.
3. Stir in okra and cook for another 1 hour on low heat.
4. Mix all the roux Ingredients: and add them to the Crockpot.
5. Stir cook on high heat until the sauce thickens.
6. Garnish as desired.
7. Serve warm.

Crack Chicken

Preparation Time: 15 minutes
Cooking Time: 4 hours
Serves: 2

Ingredients:

- ½ cup chicken broth
- 1 packet ranch seasoning
- 2 lb. chicken breast fillets
- 8 oz. cream cheese
- 8 slices bacon, cooked crispy and crumbled
- ½ cup cheddar cheese, shredded

Method:

1. Pour chicken broth into your slow cooker.
2. Add the ranch seasoning and chicken breast.
3. Stir well.
4. Cover the pot and cook on high for 4 hours.
5. Shred the chicken using two forks.
6. Put shredded chicken back to the pot.
7. Stir in the rest of the ingredients.
8. Cook for 10 more minutes.

Aromatic Jalapeno Wings

Preparation Time: 10 minutes
Cooking Time: 3 hours
Serves: 2

Ingredients:

- 1 jalapeño pepper, diced
- ½ cup of fresh cilantro, diced
- 3 tablespoon of coconut oil
- Juice from 1 lime
- 2 garlic cloves, peeled and minced
- Salt and black pepper ground, to taste
- 2 lbs. chicken wings
- Lime wedges, to serve
- Mayonnaise, to serve

Method:

1.Start by throwing all the Ingredients: into the large bowl and mix well.
2.Cover the wings and marinate them in the refrigerator for 2 hours.
3.Now add the wings along with their marinade into the Crockpot.
4.Cover it and cook for 3 hours on Low Settings.
5.Garnish as desired.
6.Serve warm.

Tuscan Garlic Chicken

Preparation Time: 15 minutes
Cooking Time: 3 hours
Serves: 2

Ingredients:

- 1 tablespoon olive oil
- 6 cloves garlic, crushed and minced
- ½ cup chicken broth
- 1 cup heavy cream
- ¾ cup Parmesan cheese, grated
- 4 chicken breasts
- 1 tablespoon Italian seasoning
- Salt and pepper to taste
- ½ cup sundried tomatoes, chopped
- 2 cups spinach, chopped

Method:

1. Pour the oil into your pan over medium heat.
2. Cook the garlic for 1 minute.
3. Stir in the broth and cream.
4. Simmer for 10 minutes.
5. Stir in the Parmesan cheese and remove from heat.
6. Put the chicken in your slow cooker.
7. Season with the salt, pepper and Italian seasoning.
8. Place the tomatoes on top of the chicken.
9. Pour the cream mixture on top of the chicken.
10. Cover the pot.
11. Cook on high for 3 hours.
12. Take the chicken out of the slow cooker and set aside.
13. Add the spinach and stir until wilted.
14. Pour the sauce over the chicken and serve with the sun-dried tomatoes and spinach.

Cider-Braised Chicken

Preparation Time: 10 minutes
Cooking Time: 5 hours
Serves: 2

Ingredients:

- 4 chicken drumsticks
- 2 tablespoon of olive oil
- ½ cup of apple cider vinegar
- 1 tablespoon of balsamic vinegar
- 1 chili pepper, diced
- 1 yellow onion, minced
- Salt and black pepper- to taste

Method:

1. Start by throwing all the Ingredients: into a bowl and mix them well.
2. Marinate this chicken for 2 hours in the refrigerator.
3. Spread the chicken along with its marinade in the Crockpot.
4. Cover it and cook for 5 hours on Low Settings.
5. Garnish as desired.
6. Serve warm.

CHAPTER 6: BEEF, PORK AND LAMB

Beef Stroganoff

Preparation Time: 15 minutes
Cooking Time: 6 hours
Serves: 2

Ingredients:

- 1 onion, sliced into wedges
- 2 cloves garlic, crushed
- 2 slices bacon, diced
- 1 lb. stewing steak, sliced into cubes
- 1 teaspoon smoked paprika
- 3 tablespoons tomato paste
- 250 ml. beef stock
- 1 cup mushrooms, sliced into quarters

Method:

1. Put all the ingredients in your slow cooker.
2. Mix well.
3. Cook on high for 6 hours.

Carnitas

Preparation Time: 15 minutes
Cooking Time: 8 hours
Serves: 2

Ingredients:

- 2 tablespoons butter
- 1 onion, sliced
- 4 tablespoons garlic, minced
- 8 lb. pork butt, sliced with crisscross pattern on top
- 2 tablespoons cumin
- 2 tablespoons thyme
- 2 tablespoons chili powder
- Salt and pepper to taste
- 1 cup water

Method:

1.Add the butter to your slow cooker.
2.Arrange the onion and garlic on the bottom of the pot.
3.Rub the pork with the spices, salt and pepper.
4.Put the meat inside the pot.
5.Add the water.
6.Cover the pot.
7.Cook on high for 8 hours.
8.Shred the meat and serve.

Meatballs

Preparation Time: 10 minutes
Cooking Time: 4 hours
Serves: 2

Ingredients:

• Olive oil
• 1 lb. ground beef
• 1 lb. ground pork
• 1 egg
• ¼ cup mayonnaise
• ¼ cup pork rinds, crushed
• 2 tablespoons Parmesan cheese, grated
• Salt and pepper to taste
For the sauce
• 14 oz. chili sauce
• 12 oz. grape jam

Method:

1. Preheat your oven to 400.
2. Drizzle baking sheet with olive oil.
3. Combine the ground beef, pork, egg, mayo, pork rinds, cheese, salt and pepper.
4. Form into meatballs.
5. Bake in the oven for 15 minutes.
6. Add the sauce ingredients to the slow cooker.
7. Mix well.
8. Add the meatballs.
9. Cover the pot and cook on low for 8 hours.

Beef Curry

Preparation Time: 10 minutes
Cooking Time: 8 hours and 10 minutes
Serves: 2

Ingredients:

- 250 ml coconut cream
- 1 teaspoon Chinese five spice
- 1 teaspoon turmeric
- ½ teaspoon chili powder
- 1 teaspoon ground cardamom
- 2 teaspoons ground coriander
- 4 cloves whole
- 1 teaspoon ground cinnamon
- 1 teaspoon ground cumin
- 1 onion, sliced into quarters
- 6 cups beef, sliced into thin strips
- 2 cups leafy greens

Method:

1. Add the coconut cream along with all the spices into your slow cooker.
2. Mix well.
3. Add the beef and onion.
4. Toss to coat evenly.
5. Cover the pot.
6. Cook on low for 8 hours.
7. Stir in the leafy greens 5 minutes before the cooking is done.

Beef Pot Roast

Preparation Time: 15 minutes
Cooking Time: 3 hours and 15 minutes
Serves: 2

Ingredients:

- 3 lb. chuck roast
- 1 teaspoon garlic powder
- Salt and pepper to taste
- ¼ cup balsamic vinegar
- 2 cups water
- ½ cup onion, chopped
- ¼ teaspoon xanthan gum
- Parsley, chopped

Method:

1. Sprinkle both sides of the chuck roast with garlic powder, salt and pepper.
2. In a pan over medium high heat, sear the roast until brown on both sides.
3. Pour the vinegar to deglaze the pan. Cook for 1 minute.
4. Transfer to your slow cooker.
5. Stir in the onion and water.
6. Boil and then cook on low for 3 hours.
7. Stir in the xanthan gum and simmer until sauce has thickened.
8. Garnish with parsley.

Pork Curry

Preparation Time: 10 minutes
Cooking Time: 10 hours
Serves: 2

Ingredients:

- 2 lb. pork belly
- 13 oz. coconut cream
- 14 oz. diced tomatoes
- ¼ teaspoon ground cloves
- ¼ teaspoon ground ginger
- ½ teaspoon granulated garlic
- 1 ½ teaspoon curry powder
- ½ teaspoon onion powder
- 2 teaspoons garam masala
For the dry rub:
- ½ teaspoon onion powder
- ½ teaspoon ground ginger
- ½ teaspoon ground cloves
- 1 tablespoon granulated garlic
- ½ teaspoon curry powder
- Salt and pepper to taste

Method:

1. Score the pork belly.
2. Mix all the dry rub ingredients in a bowl.
3. Season pork belly with this mixture.
4. Marinate in the refrigerator while covered for 2 hours.
5. In another bowl, mix the rest of the ingredients.
6. Pour the mixture into the slow cooker.
7. Add the pork belly.
8. Toss to coat evenly.
9. Cook on high for 10 hours, stirring occasionally.

Pork Roast with Creamy Gravy

Preparation Time: 15 minutes
Cooking Time: 8 hours and 15 minutes
Serves: 2

Ingredients:

- 2 lb. pork shoulder
- Salt and pepper to taste
- 1 ½ cups heavy whipping cream
- 2 teaspoons dried rosemary
- 5 black peppercorns
- 1 bay leaf
- 1 cup water
- 1 tablespoon coconut oil
- 2 cloves garlic, chopped
- 1 ½ oz. fresh ginger, grated
- 1 tablespoon arrowroot starch

Method:

1. Season pork with salt and pepper.
2. Add to a slow cooker.
3. Pour in the water.
4. Add the rosemary, peppercorns and bay leaf.
5. Cover the pot.
6. Cook on low for 8 hours.
7. Take it out of the pot and transfer to a plate.
8. In a bowl, combine the oil, garlic and ginger.
9. Rub pork with this mixture.
10. Bake in the oven for 15 minutes.
11. Get the cooking liquid from the pot.
12. Mix with the arrowroot starch.
13. Slice the beef and pour gravy on top before serving.

Lamb Shanks with Green Beans

Preparation Time: 20 minutes
Cooking Time: 8 hours and 10 minutes
Serves: 2

Ingredients:

- 6 lamb shanks
- 1 tablespoon olive oil
- Salt and pepper to taste
- 2 carrots, chopped
- 2 stalks celery, chopped
- 1 onion, chopped
- 1 tablespoon dried oregano
- 1 cup red wine
- 1 ½ cups chicken stock
- 1 ½ tablespoons rosemary
- 1 cup crushed tomatoes
- 3 bay leaves
- 3 cups green beans, sliced
- 1 tablespoon olive oil

Method:

1. In a skillet, pour the oil and cook the lamb shanks until brown on all sides.
2. Transfer to a plate.
3. Add the vegetables and cook for 5 minutes.
4. Transfer to a slow cooker.
5. Pour the red wine into the pan to deglaze.
6. Transfer to the slow cooker.
7. Add all the spices, chicken stock and tomatoes to the pot.
8. Stir in the lamb shanks.
9. Cover the pot.
10. Cook on low for 8 hours.
11. Sauté the green beans in oil.
12. Serve the lamb shanks with the beans.

Beef & Broccoli

Preparation Time: 10 minutes
Cooking Time: 6 hours
Serves: 2

Ingredients:

- 2/3 cup liquid amino
- 2 lb. flank steak, sliced into strips
- 3 tablespoons stevia
- 1 cup beef broth
- 3 cloves garlic, minced
- 1 teaspoon ginger, grated
- Salt to taste
- ½ teaspoon red pepper flakes
- 2 cups broccoli florets
- 1 red bell pepper, sliced into strips

Method:

1. Add all the ingredients except broccoli and red bell pepper into the slow cooker.
2. Seal the pot.
3. Cook low for 6 hours.
4. Stir in the broccoli and red bell pepper.
5. Cook for another 1 hour.

Beef Short Ribs

Preparation Time: 5 minutes
Cooking Time: 8 hours
Serves: 2

Ingredients:

- 1 tablespoon olive oil
- 2 lb. beef short ribs
- ½ cup beef broth
- 3 oz. cream cheese
- 1 teaspoon garlic powder
- 2 cups white mushrooms
- Salt and pepper to taste

Method:

1.Place the skillet in medium heat.
2.Add the oil and cook the ribs until brown.
3.Mix the rest of the ingredients in your slow cooker.
4.Seal the pot. Cook on low for 8 hours. Mix every 2 hours.

Mongolian Beef

Preparation Time: 10 minutes
Cooking Time: 6 hours
Serves: 2

Ingredients:

- 1 ½ lb. sirloin steak, sliced
- ¼ cup sugar
- ¼ cup water
- ¼ cup soy sauce
- 2 cloves garlic, crushed and minced
- 2 tablespoons sesame oil
- ¼ teaspoon red pepper flakes
- ½ teaspoon ground ginger
- ¼ teaspoon xanthan gum
- 2 green onion, chopped

Method:

1. Add the beef to the slow cooker.
2. In a bowl, mix the brown sugar, water, soy sauce, garlic, oil, red pepper flakes and ginger.
3. Pour this mixture over the beef.
4. Cover the pot.
5. Cook on low for 6 hours.
6. Take out a tablespoon of the cooking liquid.
7. Add xanthan gum to the liquid.
8. Pour this mixture back to the pot.
9. Sprinkle green onion on top.

Barbecue Pulled Pork

Preparation Time: 15 minutes
Cooking Time: 6 hours
Serves: 2

Ingredients:

- ¼ cup white wine vinegar
- 2 teaspoons olive oil
- 3 teaspoons paprika
- 2 teaspoons dried oregano
- 2 teaspoons garlic powder
- Salt and pepper to taste
- ¾ teaspoons ground cumin
- 1 teaspoon chipotle powder
- ¼ teaspoon cayenne pepper
- 1 tablespoon erythritol
- 2 lb. pork shoulder, sliced into cubes
- 1 tablespoon olive oil
- 1 tablespoon orange juice
- 1 teaspoon arrowroot powder

Method:

1.Mix all the ingredients except orange juice and arrowroot powder.
2.Put the mixture into the slow cooker.
3.Cover the pot and cook on low for 6 hours.
4.Stir in orange juice and arrowroot powder.
5.Shred the meat and serve with the sauce.

Pulled Pork

Preparation Time: 5 minutes
Cooking Time: 8 hours
Serves: 2

Ingredients:

- 3 lb. boneless pork shoulder
- 1 tablespoon parsley
- 2 teaspoons cumin
- 2 teaspoons garlic powder
- 2 teaspoons onion powder
- Salt to taste
- 2 teaspoons paprika
- ½ cup beer

Method:

1. Put the pork shoulder to your slow cooker.
2. In a bowl, mix all the spices and herbs with the salt.
3. Rub pork with this mixture.
4. Add beer to the slow cooker.
5. Cover your pot.
6. Cook on low for 8 hours.
7. Shred the meat with fork.
8. Serve warm.

Spicy Pork Chops

Preparation Time: 5 minutes
Cooking Time: 8 hours
Serves: 2

Ingredients:

- 1 tablespoon dried thyme
- 1 tablespoon dried rosemary
- 1 tablespoon chives, chopped
- 1 tablespoon curry powder
- 1 tablespoon ground cumin
- 1 tablespoon fennel seeds
- Salt to taste
- 4 tablespoons olive oil, divided
- 2 lb. pork chops

Method:

1. In a bowl, mix all the spices with salt and 1 tablespoon olive oil.
2. Rub pork chops with this mixture.
3. Place the meat to your slow cooker.
4. Pour in the remaining oil.
5. Cook on high for 8 hours.

Lamb with Thyme

Preparation Time: 5 minutes
Cooking Time: 3 hours
Serves: 2

Ingredients:

- 2 lamb chops, trimmed
- 1 cup vegetable stock
- ½ cup red wine
- 1 teaspoon garlic paste
- ¼ cup fresh thyme
- Salt and pepper to taste

Method:

1. Add all the ingredients in your slow cooker. Mix well.
2. Cover and cook on high for 3 hours.
3. Pour sauce over the lamb before serving.

CHAPTER 7: SEAFOOD AND FISH

Lemon Salmon

Preparation Time: 10 minutes
Cooking Time: 2 hours
Serves: 2

Ingredients:

- 2 lbs. skin-on salmon fillets
- Salt, to taste
- Fresh black pepper to taste
- 1 lemon, sliced
- ¼ cup of onion
- ¼ cup of fennel
- 1 to 1 1/2 cups of water

Method:

1.Start by throwing all the Ingredients: into your Crockpot.
2.Cover its lid and cook for 2 hours on Low setting.
3.Once done, remove its lid and give it a stir.
4.Serve warm.

Seafood Stew

Preparation Time: 10 minutes
Cooking Time: 2.5 hours
Serves: 2

Ingredients:

- 1 can (28 oz.) Crushed tomatoes
- 1 tablespoon of tomato paste
- 4 cups of vegetable broth
- 3 garlic cloves, minced
- 1/2 cup of diced white onion
- 1 teaspoon of thyme, dried
- 1 teaspoon of dried basil
- 1 teaspoon of oregano, dried
- 1/2 teaspoon of celery salt
- 1/4 teaspoon of crushed red pepper flakes
- 1/8 teaspoon of cayenne pepper
- Salt and pepper to taste
- 1 lb. large shrimp
- 1 lb. scallops
- A handful of fresh parsley, chopped

Method:

1. Start by throwing all the Ingredients: into your Crockpot except seafood.
2. Cover its lid and cook for 2 hours on Low setting.
3. Once done, remove its lid and give it a stir.
4. Stir in seafood and continue cooking for 30 minutes on low heat.
5. Serve warm.

Shrimp Scampi

Preparation Time: 15 minutes
Cooking Time: 3 hours
Serves: 2

Ingredients:

- ¼ cup chicken bone broth
- ½ cup white cooking wine
- 2 tablespoons olive oil
- 2 tablespoons butter
- 1 tablespoon garlic, minced
- 2 tablespoons parsley, chopped
- 1 tablespoon lemon juice
- Salt and pepper to taste
- 1 lb. shrimp, peeled and deveined

Method:

1. Mix all the ingredients in your slow cooker.
2. Cover the pot.
3. Cook on low for 3 hours.

Elegant Dinner Mussels

Preparation Time: 10 minutes
Cooking Time: 2 hours
Serves: 2

Ingredients:

- 2 lbs. mussels, cleaned and de-bearded
- 2 tablespoons of butter
- 1 medium yellow onion, diced
- 1 garlic clove, minced
- ½ teaspoon of rosemary, dried, crushed
- 1 cup of homemade chicken broth
- 2 tablespoons of fresh lemon juice
- ½ cup of sour cream
- Salt and black pepper, to taste

Method:

1. Start by throwing all the Ingredients: into your Crockpot except cream.
2. Cover its lid and cook for 2 hours on High setting.
3. Once done, remove its lid and give it a stir.
4. Stir in cream and mix it all gently
5. Serve warm.

Fish Curry

Preparation Time: 10 minutes
Cooking Time: 2 hours
Serves: 2

Ingredients:

- 1 lb. salmon fillets, cut into bite-sized pieces
- 1 curry leaves
- ½ tablespoon of olive oil
- ½ teaspoon of red chili powder
- ½ small yellow onion, diced
- 1 garlic clove, minced
- 1 tablespoon of curry powder
- 1 teaspoon of cumin, ground
- 1 teaspoon of ground coriander
- ½ teaspoon of ground turmeric
- 1 cup of unsweetened coconut milk
- 1 cups of tomato, diced
- ½ Serrano pepper, seeded and diced
- ½ tablespoon of fresh lemon juice

Method:

1.Start by throwing all the Ingredients: into your Crockpot.
2.Cover its lid and cook for 2 hours on High setting.
3.Once done, remove its lid and give it a stir.
4.Serve warm.

Shrimp & Sausage Gumbo

Preparation Time: 15 minutes
Cooking Time: 1 hour and 15 minutes
Serves: 2

Ingredients:

- 3 tablespoons olive oil
- 2 lb. chicken thigh fillet, sliced into cubes
- 4 cloves garlic, crushed and minced
- 1 onion, sliced
- 3 stalks celery, chopped
- 1 green bell pepper, chopped
- 1 teaspoon Cajun seasoning
- Salt to taste
- 2 cups beef broth
- 28 oz. canned crushed tomatoes
- 12 oz. sausage
- 2 tablespoons butter
- 1 lb. shrimp, peeled and deveined

Method:

1. Pour the olive oil in a pan over medium heat.
2. Cook the garlic and chicken for 5 minutes.
3. Add the onion, celery and bell pepper.
4. Cook until tender.
5. Season with the Cajun seasoning and salt.
6. Cook for 2 minutes.
7. Stir in the sausage, broth and tomatoes.
8. Cover and cook on low for 1 hour.
9. Add the butter and shrimp in the last 10 minutes of cooking.

Shrimp Boil

Preparation Time: 15 minutes
Cooking Time: 4 hours
Serves: 2

Ingredients:

- 1 ½ lb. potatoes, sliced into wedges
- 6 cloves garlic, peeled
- 3 ears corn
- 1 lb. sausage, sliced
- ¼ cup Old Bay seasoning
- 1 tablespoon lemon juice
- 6 cups water
- 2 lb. shrimp, peeled

Method:

1. Put the potatoes in your slow cooker.
2. Add the garlic, corn and sausage in layers.
3. Season with the Old Bay seasoning.
4. Drizzle lemon juice on top.
5. Pour in the water.
6. Do not mix.
7. Cover the pot.
8. Cook on high for 4 hours.
9. Add the shrimp on top.
10. Cook for 15 minutes.

Curried Shrimp

Preparation Time: 10 minutes
Cooking Time: 2.5 hours
Serves: 2

Ingredients:

- 1 tablespoon of olive oil
- 1 medium onion, diced
- ½ teaspoon of cumin, ground
- 1½ teaspoons of red chili powder
- 1 teaspoon of ground turmeric
- Pinch of salt
- 2 medium tomatoes, diced
- ¼ cup of water
- 1¾ lbs. medium shrimp, peeled and deveined
- 1 tablespoon of fresh lemon juice
- ¼ cup of fresh cilantro, diced

Method:

1. Start by throwing all the Ingredients: into your Crockpot except shrimp.
2. Cover its lid and cook for 2 hours on Low setting.
3. Once done, remove its lid and give it a stir.
4. Add shrimp and continue cooking for 30 minutes on low heat.
5. Serve warm.

Seafood Bisque

Preparation Time: 15 minutes
Cooking Time: 2 hours and 35 minutes
Serves: 2

Ingredients:

• 2 tablespoons coconut oil
• ¼ cup onion, diced
• 1 stalk celery, diced
• 1 leek, sliced
• 1 teaspoon orange zest
• 1 teaspoon fresh thyme
• 8 oz. cream cheese
• 3 cups chicken broth
• 2 tablespoons tomato paste
• Salt and pepper to taste
• 12 oz. shrimp, cooked

Method:

1.Add oil to a skillet over medium heat.
2.Cook the onion, celery, leek, orange zest and thyme for 4 minutes.
3.Transfer to a slow cooker.
4.Stir in the rest of the ingredients except the shrimp.
5.Cover the pot and cook on low for 2 hours.
6.Stir in the shrimp 30 minutes before cooking is done.

Salmon with Lemon & Dill

Preparation Time: 15 minutes
Cooking Time: 2 hours
Serves: 2

Ingredients:

- Cooking spray
- 1 teaspoon olive oil
- 2 lb. salmon
- 1 tablespoon fresh dill, chopped
- Salt and pepper to taste
- 1 clove garlic, minced
- 1 lemon, sliced

Method:

1.Spray your slow cooker with oil.
2.Brush both sides of salmon with olive oil.
3.Season the salmon with salt, pepper, dill and garlic.
4.Add to the slow cooker.
5.Put the lemon slices on top.
6.Cover the pot and cook on high for 2 hours.

Salmon with Lemon Cream Sauce

Preparation Time: 10 minutes
Cooking Time: 2 hours and 20 minutes
Serves: 2

Ingredients:

For the salmon
- 3 lemons, sliced and divided
- 2 lb. salmon fillet
- Cooking spray
- Salt and pepper to taste
- ½ teaspoon sweet paprika
- ½ teaspoon chili powder
- 1 teaspoon garlic powder
- 1 teaspoon Italian Seasoning
- 1 cup vegetable broth
- 1 tablespoon lemon juice
For the sauce
- 3 tablespoons lemon juice
- ¼ cup chicken broth
- 2/3 cup heavy cream
- Lemon zest

Method:

1. Cover slow cooker with parchment paper.
2. Arrange the lemon slices in the middle.
3. Put the salmon fillet on top.
4. Spray salmon with oil and season with herbs and spices.
5. Pour the lemon juice and broth into the slow cooker around and not on top of the fish.
6. Cover and cook on low for 2 hours.
7. Combine the sauce ingredients.
8. Stir into the pot.
9. Set it to low and cook for 8 minutes.
10. Garnish with the zest.

Fish Stew

Preparation Time: 15 minutes
Cooking Time: 1 hour and 24 minutes
Serves: 2

Ingredients:

- 1 lb. white fish
- 1 tablespoon lime juice
- 1 onion, sliced
- 2 cloves garlic, sliced
- 1 red pepper, sliced
- 1 jalapeno pepper, sliced
- 1 teaspoon paprika
- 2 cups chicken broth
- 2 cups tomatoes, chopped
- Salt and pepper to taste
- 15 oz. coconut milk

Method:

1.Marinate the fish in lime juice for 10 minutes.
2.Pour the olive oil into a pan over medium heat.
3.Add the onion, garlic and peppers.
4.Cook for 4 minutes.
5.Add the rest of the ingredients except the coconut milk.
6.Cover the pot.
7.Cook on low for 1 hour.
8.Stir in the coconut milk and simmer for 10 minutes.

Shrimp Jambalaya

Preparation Time: 10 minutes
Cooking Time: 8 hours
Serves: 2

Ingredients:

- 1 lb. sausage, sliced
- 1 lb. chicken breast fillets, sliced into cubes
- 1 onion, chopped
- 1 cup celery, chopped
- 1 green pepper, chopped
- 28 oz. canned diced tomatoes
- 1 cup chicken broth
- 2 teaspoons parsley, chopped
- 2 teaspoons fresh oregano, chopped
- 1 teaspoon cayenne pepper
- 2 teaspoons Cajun seasoning
- 1 lb. shrimp, peeled
- ½ teaspoon fresh thyme, chopped
- Salt and pepper to taste

Method:

1. Put all the ingredients except the shrimp in a slow cooker.
2. Mix well.
3. Cook low for 8 hours.
4. Stir in the shrimp 30 minutes before cooking is done.

Lobster Dinner

Preparation Time: 10 minutes
Cooking Time: 1 hour
Serves: 2

Ingredients:

- 2 lbs. lobster tails, cut in half
- 2 tablespoons of unsalted butter, melted
- Pinch of salt
- 2 oz. white wine
- 4 oz. water

Method:

1. Start by throwing all the Ingredients: into your Crockpot.
2. Cover its lid and cook for 1 hour on Low setting.
3. Once done, remove its lid and give it a stir.
4. Serve warm.

CHAPTER 8: DESSERTS

Pineapple Cheese Cake

Preparation Time: 15 minutes
Cooking Time: 6 hours
Serves: 2

Ingredients:

- 8oz. cream cheese
- 8oz. ricotta cheese
- 1 tablespoon of sugar-free pineapple extract
- ¼ cup of erythritol
- 2 eggs
- ¼ cup of sour cream
- 1 tablespoon of vanilla extract
- 2 cups of mixed nuts, crushed
- 2 tablespoons of unsalted butter, melted
- ¼ cup of raspberries

Method:

1. Start by blending the Nuts with butter in the mixer.
2. Spread this Nuts mixture in the greased Crockpot firmly.
3. Now beat the remaining filling Ingredients: except berries in a blender until smooth.
4. Add this cream filling to the Nutty crust and spread evenly.
5. Cover its lid and cook for 6 hours on Low setting.
6. Once done, remove its lid of the crockpot carefully.
7. Allow it to cool and refrigerate for 12 hours.
8. Garnish with berries.
9. Serve.

Caramel Cheesecake

Preparation Time: 15 minutes
Cooking Time: 6 hours
Serves: 2

Ingredients:

• 8oz. cream cheese
• ¼ cup of erythritol
• 2 eggs
• ¼ cup of sour cream
• 1 tablespoon of vanilla extract
• 2 cups of mixed nuts, crushed
• 2 tablespoons of unsalted butter, melted
Toppings:
• 10 caramels, unwrapped
• 2 tablespoons of heavy cream
• ¼ cup of melted sugar-free chocolate

Method:

1. Start by blending the Nuts with butter in the mixer.
2. Spread this Nuts mixture in the greased Crockpot firmly.
3. Now beat the remaining filling Ingredients: except berries in a blender until smooth.
4. Add this cream filling to the Nutty crust and spread evenly.
5. Cover its lid and cook for 6 hours on Low setting.
6. Once done, remove its lid of the crockpot carefully.
7. Allow it to cool and refrigerate for 1 hour.
8. Garnish with berries and other toppings.
9. Serve.

Chocolate Cream Custard

Preparation Time: 15 minutes
Cooking Time: 2 hours
Serves: 2

Ingredients:

- 4 cups of almond milk
- 6 eggs
- 3/4 cup of brown swerve
- 1 teaspoon of vanilla extract
- 1 teaspoon of cocoa powder
- ¼ teaspoon of cinnamon, ground
- Sugar-free chocolate, grated
- Whipped cream

Method:

1.Start by blending all the Ingredients: together in a mixer.
2.Pour this mixture into 4 ramekins and place them in the Crockpot.
3.Cover its lid and cook for 2 hours on Low setting.
4.Once done, remove its lid of the crockpot carefully.
5.Allow it to cool and refrigerate for 1 hour.
6.Garnish with chocolate and whipped cream.
7.Serve.

Raspberry Custard Trifle

Preparation Time: 15 minutes
Cooking Time: 3 hours
Serves: 2

Ingredients:

• 4 cups of almond milk
• 6 eggs
• 3/4 cup of erythritol
• 1 teaspoon of vanilla extract
• 1 pinch salt
• ¼ teaspoon of cinnamon, ground
• 4 tablespoons of brown swerve
• 2 tablespoons of water
• 1 cup of raspberries

Method:

1. Start by blending all the Ingredients: together in a mixer except raspberries, brown swerve, and water.
2. Pour this mixture into 4 ramekins and place them in the Crockpot.
3. Cover its lid and cook for 3 hours on Low setting.
4. Once done, remove its lid of the crockpot carefully.
5. Allow it to cool and refrigerate for 1 hour.
6. Meanwhile, boil brown swerve with water in a saucepan and cook until it is caramelized.
7. Garnish the custard with raspberries then pour the caramel mixture on top.
8. Serve.

Berry Mix

Preparation Time: 5 minutes
Cooking Time: 2 hours
Serves: 2

Ingredients:

- Cooking spray
- 2 cups frozen strawberries
- 2 cups frozen blackberries
- 2 cups frozen blueberries
- 1 tablespoon orange juice
- 1 teaspoon orange zest
- 2 tablespoons water

Method:

1. Spray your crockpot with oil.
2. Add all the ingredients in the pot.
3. Cover the pot.
4. Cook on low for 2 hours.

Fruit Medley

Preparation Time: 10 minutes
Cooking Time: 1 hour
Serves: 2

Ingredients:

• 1 cup frozen cherries
• 1 cup dried cranberries
• 1 cup frozen strawberries
• 1 cup frozen blueberries
• 1 teaspoon vanilla extract
• 1 teaspoon cinnamon
• 1 cup butter
• ¼ cup chopped almonds

Method:

1.Put all the ingredients except the almonds in the crockpot.
2.Seal the pot and cook on high for 1 hour.
3.Sprinkle almonds on top before serving.

Fruit Salad

Preparation Time: 10 minutes
Cooking Time: 2 hours
Serves: 2

Ingredients:

- ¾ cup sugar
- ½ cup butter
- ¼ teaspoon ground cinnamon
- ¼ teaspoon ground nutmeg
- Salt to taste
- 15 oz. peaches, sliced
- ½ cup dried apricots
- ½ cup dried blackberries
- Chopped walnuts

Method:

1. Combine all the ingredients except the walnuts in the crockpot.
2. Mix well.
3. Seal the pot and cook on high for 2 hours.
4. Sprinkle with the walnuts before serving.

Traditional Egg Custard

Preparation Time: 15 minutes
Cooking Time: 3 hours
Serves: 2

Ingredients:

- 4 cups of almond milk
- 6 eggs
- 3/4 cup of erythritol
- 1 teaspoon of vanilla extract
- 1 pinch salt
- ¼ teaspoon of cinnamon, ground
- Nutmeg, grated
- Fresh fruits, diced

Method:

1. Start by blending all the Ingredients: together in a mixer.
2. Pour this mixture into 4 ramekins and place them in the Crockpot.
3. Cover its lid and cook for 2-3 hours on Low setting.
4. Once done, remove its lid of the crockpot carefully.
5. Allow it to cool and refrigerate for 1 hour.
6. Garnish as desired.
7. Serve.

Fruit Crisp

Preparation Time: 4 hours
Cooking Time: 15 minutes
Serves: 2

Ingredients:

- 6 cups apples, sliced
- 1 cup dried cranberries
- 1 teaspoon orange zest
- 5 teaspoons ground cinnamon
- 1 cup quick oats
- 1 teaspoon dried ginger
- ¾ cup butter

Method:

1. Stir all the ingredients in the crockpot.
2. Cook on high for 1 hour.

Fruity Custard Delight

Preparation Time: 15 minutes
Cooking Time: 4 hours
Serves: 2

Ingredients:

• 4 cups of almond milk
• 6 eggs
• 3/4 cup of brown swerve
• 1 teaspoon of vanilla extract
• 1 pinch salt
• ¼ teaspoon of cinnamon, ground
To serve:
• 1 cup of whipped cream
• 1 lb. keto sponge cake, sliced
• Mix berries, sliced

Method:

1.Start by blending all the Ingredients: together in a mixer.
2.Pour this mixture into a steel pan and place it in the Crockpot.
3.Cover its lid and cook for 4 hours on Low setting.
4.Once done, remove its lid of the crockpot carefully.
5.Allow it to cool and refrigerate for 1 hour.
6.To serve, layer a casserole dish with sponge cake slices.
7.Top them with prepared custard and garnish with fresh fruits.
8.Refrigerate again for 4 hours or more.
9.Serve.

Peach & Blackberry

Preparation Time: 20 minutes
Cooking Time: 3 hours
Serves: 2

Ingredients:

- 1 cup rolled oats
- 2 teaspoons ground cinnamon
- 1 teaspoon ground nutmeg
- ½ cup butter
- Cooking spray
- 3 lb. peaches, sliced
- 3 cups blackberries
- Walnuts, chopped

Method:

1.Combine all the ingredients except walnuts in a bowl.
2.Transfer to your crockpot.
3.Spray your pot with oil.
4.Cover and cook on low for 3 hours.
5.Sprinkle walnuts on top.

Winter Fruits

Preparation Time: 10 minutes
Cooking Time: 6 hours
Serves: 2

Ingredients:

- 1 cinnamon stick
- 2 apples, sliced
- ¼ cup dried cranberries
- ¼ cup raisins
- ½ cup dried apricots
- 8 oz. pineapple chunks
- ¾ cup orange juice

Method:

1. Add all the ingredients in your crockpot.
2. Seal the pot.
3. Cook on low setting for 6 hours.
4. Discard cinnamon stick before serving.

Cinnamon Strawberries

Preparation Time: 5 minutes
Cooking Time: 1 hour
Serves: 2

Ingredients:

• 4 cups frozen strawberries
• 2 tablespoons ground cinnamon
• 1 tablespoon ground nutmeg
• 1 cup orange juice
• Flaxseed

Method:

1.Mix all the ingredients except flaxseed in your crockpot.
2.Seal the pot and cook on low for 1 hour.
3.Sprinkle flaxseed on top before serving.

Spiced Peaches

Preparation Time: 10 minutes
Cooking Time: 4 hours
Serves: 2

Ingredients:

• Cooking spray
• 4 cups frozen peaches, sliced
• 1 teaspoon ground cinnamon
• ½ teaspoon ground nutmeg
• 1 teaspoon vanilla extract
• ½ cup almond milk

Method:

1.Spray your slow cooker with oil.
2.In a bowl, mix all the ingredients.
3.Transfer to the pot.
4.Cover and cook on low for 3 hours.

CONCLUSION

A crock pot is an electrical device that you can place on your counter, plugin, and start cooking. You can eat delicious and healthy meals despite your busy schedule if you have a crock pot. Crock Pot Cookbook for Two is the book for you. This cookbook includes healthy crock pot recipes without sacrificing your precious time.

Basics of healthy crock pot recipes are what this cookbook distributes. Take a closer look into these slow cooker recipes, you might find yourself wondering how on earth have you been cooking without them all this time.

So are you ready to get started? Good luck!

Printed in the USA
CPSIA information can be obtained
at www.ICGtesting.com
LVHW080718161023
761142LV00057B/28